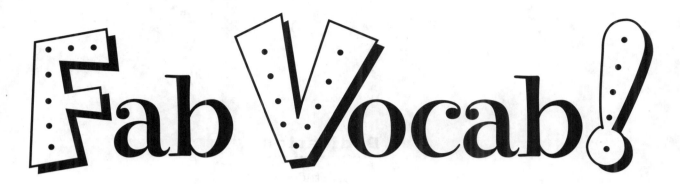

Fab Vocab!

35 Creative Vocabulary-Boosting Activities for Kids of All Learning Styles

by Marguerite Hartill

whimsical
captivating
articulate

SCHOLASTIC
PROFESSIONAL BOOKS

New York • Toronto • London • Auckland • Sydney

Dedication

To my students

Cover design by Jaime Lucero and Vincent Ceci
Cover photographs by Donnelly Marks
Interior design by Sydney Wright
Interior illustrations by Sydney Wright

ISBN 0-590-76251-6
Copyright © 1998 by Marguerite Hartill

Contents

PART III

Vocabulary Review, Projects, and Year-End Wrap-ups

whimsical · pseudonym · audacious · genial · premonition · cryptic

Introduction

Many years ago my seventh-grade English teacher told our class that we had to use our vocabulary words 17 times before we could call them our own. She said that then and only then could we feel comfortable knowing they would be there when it came time to use them. She promised that we would be able to impress teachers, friends, and even parents when we used the vocabulary words in compositions and reports.

I thought that was a pretty tall order at the tender age of 12, and I didn't give it too much credence. It was just another technique a teacher had developed to convince her students to learn, I thought. To tell the truth, I really don't remember the methods she used to teach vocabulary in her class. Sorry, Miss Andresen, it's been a very long time. Her statement, however, has stayed in the back of my mind for decades.

In college I read a study about repetitive motion. It stated that anything done 17 times would become habit. My English teacher was right! It was funny how her remark, made many years ago, leaped into the present. I made the connection, and suddenly it made sense.

articulate • enterprising • adage • frivolous • accord • metaphor

Years later, after I began teaching vocabulary from a very traditional but boring vocabulary workbook (I won't mention the name), I began to wonder if there were other ways to help my students really learn those words. Doing rote exercises from a workbook wasn't very successful, even though the words were repeated several times in the exercises. Test grades were mediocre at best. Seventeen times popped up again. I thought that if I could find new ways for my students to use and apply their vocabulary words, it might just do the trick.

I began this new venture with a few activities and methods I thought would work. They did. Over the years I've added other ideas. I've shared those ideas with my colleagues and they've been happy with the results. My students' test grades began to rise, and I was overjoyed—17 times to be exact.

If you're like me and are required to use a vocabulary book (or list), let your students do the exercises from the book for homework. Read the correct answers the next day in class and answer any questions. Then begin the fun part. Starting with any of the activities in this book, have students spend five to ten minutes each day using their vocabulary words in different writing exercises and activities. Students will need to adjust to this spontaneous writing, and it may take more time at first. But as they settle in and expect to write, they will be able to do so within the allotted time period. Or you may want to devote half a period twice a week to your vocabulary and writing activities. In any case, everyone should find a comfort zone.

As students work on an exercise or activity, I walk around and visit, peek over a few shoulders, and ask for responses to the assignment. When

denotation • captivating • waver • plausible • opus • disarming

students complete the assignment, I usually ask three or four volunteers to share their writing with the class. I also ask for copies of the very best writing for my collection. Students are pleased when I say, "I'd love a copy of your work." They always deliver it promptly.

The lessons in this book have been divided into three parts. The exercises in Part I are relatively simple and can be used to introduce new vocabulary words. The activities in Part II are designed to be used as students become more familiar with their vocabulary words. The lessons in Part III involve critical- and creative-thinking activities to help students synthesize vocabulary words with their everyday writing. They can also be used to provide a comprehensive review of vocabulary words that students have learned throughout the year.

As you work through the exercises in this book, you'll find that many of the activities challenge students to experiment with literary forms and techniques, such as writing parables and concrete poems and using alliteration. You may want to teach a mini-lesson on some of these concepts before you start the vocabulary lesson.

Good luck—17 times! I guarantee that you'll enjoy reading the results!

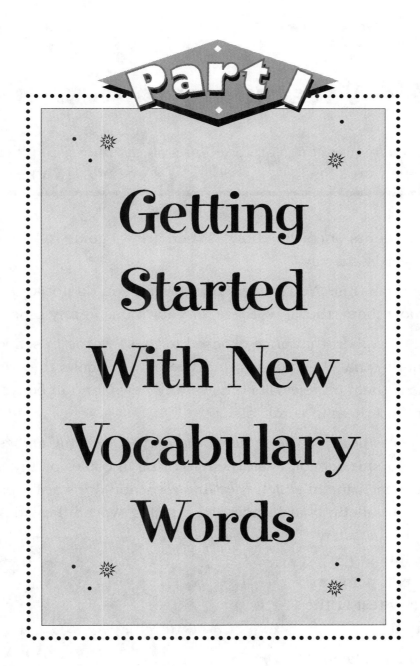

Part I

Getting Started With New Vocabulary Words

pseudonym · audacious · genial · premonition · adage · whimsical · articulate

▽ Vocabulary in Action

> The limits of my language are the limits of my mind. All I know is what I have words for. —Ludwig Wittgenstein

One of my students once asked me, "When are we going to be using all these **hard** words anyway?"

My response was this: "You'll never use them if you do not know them. If you do know them, they'll be there for you to use at any time."

I continued to explain that once exposed to these words in school, students will notice that they pop up unexpectedly in books they read. They will hear them on television shows, the news, and in conversation. They'll even find them in comic strips!

To help students begin to notice how frequently they come across vocabulary words outside school, I ask them to bring in copies of any newspaper, book, or magazine in which they find a vocabulary word. I post the examples on a bulletin board under the heading "Vocabulary in Action."

For each word a student finds, I give him or her one extra-credit point on the vocabulary test at the end of the unit.

Let your students keep track of the vocabulary words they find in the real world with the Vocabulary Word Hunt cards on page 11.

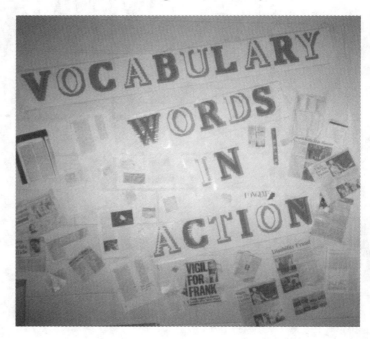

Vocabulary Word Hunt

Name .... ★ .

Vocabulary word: ....

Where I found it: ....

Definition: ....

....

The sentence the word was used in: ....

....

....

Vocabulary Word Hunt

Name .... ★ .

Vocabulary word: ....

Where I found it: ....

Definition: ....

....

The sentence the word was used in: ....

....

....

Vocabulary Word Hunt

Name .... ★

Vocabulary word: ....

Where I found it: ....

Definition: ....

....

The sentence the word was used in: ....

....

....

▽ 2 ▽ **Crossword Puzzles**

Crossword puzzles are an excellent way for students to learn new words. In my class, we begin each new vocabulary unit with a crossword puzzle. As students grapple with the new words and try to fit them into the puzzle, they learn their meaning, spelling, and pronunciation.

I create the puzzle by fitting the new vocabulary words into a grid format and supplying brief definitions or synonyms of the words for clues. You can copy the reproducible grid on page 13 to create puzzles using your vocabulary words.

After students have completed the puzzle and we've reviewed the answers, I always like to make connections between new words and words they already know. For example, the word *wrangle* is a word most students have already heard. Why? Most likely it's because they've worn Wrangler jeans or seen commercials for the Jeep Wrangler. I always explain that cowboys were the first to wear jeans and they certainly wrangled a great deal. When I make the connection to the Jeep, we talk about the way the Wrangler tackles even the highest mountain and wins. Once a word is linked to prior knowledge, it becomes easier to comprehend and remember.

◀ Taking It Further ▶

Challenge students to create their own crossword puzzles using the grid provided. You'll need to give students two copies of the grid (page 13). After writing brief clues for each word, students fit the words into the grid and number each word and the corresponding clue. On a second grid, they can number the grid and write clues for each word, leaving those squares that will be filled blank and shading in all others. Students can exchange puzzles with their classmates.

Name ....

Crossword Puzzle

Across Clues

....

....

....

....

....

....

....

Down Clues

....

....

....

....

....

....

....

3 ▽ Acrostics

Invite students to create an acrostic using one of their new vocabulary words. Students start their acrostics by writing each letter of the word down the left margin of a sheet of paper. Then they can write sentences or phrases that begin with each letter in the vocabulary word. Each sentence should help to define the word. The sentences in the acrostic can contain the vocabulary word itself or other vocabulary words. When they've completed their acrostic, students will find that it sounds like a poem or a story.

BONANZA

Bountiful stashes of hidden gold
Opulent assets and treasures
Numbers of jewels, bundles of riches
Assortment of prizes and dividends
Numbers of possessions so valuable
Zillions of dollars in wealth
Absolute prosperity and security

4 ▽ Acrostic Art

BASK
BASK
BASK

(B)athing in the sun is one of my favorite things. (A) day at the beach is the best way to spend a summer day. (S)unny days are great! (K)elly, my friend, and I love to bask in the sun.

BASK
BASK
BASK
BASK

If students want to be a little more creative with their acrostics, they can also illustrate them in a way that further explains the vocabulary word. In this example, the student highlights her acrostic about the word *bask* by writing it on a sun-shaped cutout.

⑤ ▼ Answering Machines

It seems as if everyone has an answering machine to take messages for them while they're away from home. Have students use vocabulary words to write a message for an answering machine. The machine can be their own, or it can be an answering machine for a business.

Hello! Sorry, I can't come to the phone right now. I'm not within **proximity** of it. Please leave a message for me.

Remember to speak up so you are not **inaudible**. I'll leave **ample** time for you to give any information I might need to return your call. Beep.

⑥ ▼ Write a Haiku!

Vocabulary words don't always have to be part of a report or a composition. Integrate vocabulary into a poetry unit by encouraging students to use new words creatively in a poem.

One easy and fun way to do this is to have students write a haiku with vocabulary words. A haiku is a Japanese form of poetry that traditionally features three lines—with five syllables in the first and third lines and seven syllables in the second line.

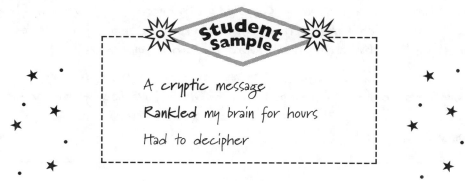

A **cryptic** message
Rankled my brain for hours
Had to **decipher**

Using Vocabulary Words in Headlines and News Stories

Connect current events with vocabulary by challenging students to write headlines and news stories using vocabulary words. Ask students to read the newspaper or watch the news on television and then create a headline about the top story of the day that includes one of their vocabulary words. As a follow-up, students can use additional vocabulary to write a news story to accompany the headline.

You can adapt this activity to fit a variety of subjects. For example:

- Students can write headlines and news stories about a historic event your class is studying.
- Students can use this format to report on the actions of a character in a novel or story.

No One Kept **Vigil** Last Night

Ivan Kovanick died last night in the Moscow Cemetery. He was found this morning with a **saber** plunged through his coat, frozen to death. Apparently, he tried to **grope** for the saber through the folds of his long coat in order to remove it, but fear captured his soul.

While searching for the facts of the story, rumors tell of a loud, **discordant** group of Russian Cossacks who challenged Ivan to a dare. They teased and taunted him, but there was no **wrangling** involved. As he left the saloon late that night, there were no **plaudits**, only jeers.

Soon the Cossacks forgot Ivan and returned to their drinking. If anyone cared enough for this poor man, he would have been found earlier and saved. Ivan should have known the old **adage**, "You have nothing to fear but fear itself."

▽⑧▽ **Creating Vocab Ads**

Advertising executives create new names for products all the time, and the product names are often derived from our everyday vocabulary—for example, the Honda *Accord*, or *Finesse* and *Pert* shampoo. Have students choose any new vocabulary word and create a product using that word as its name. Then have them write a brief advertisement for the product, using two additional vocabulary words.

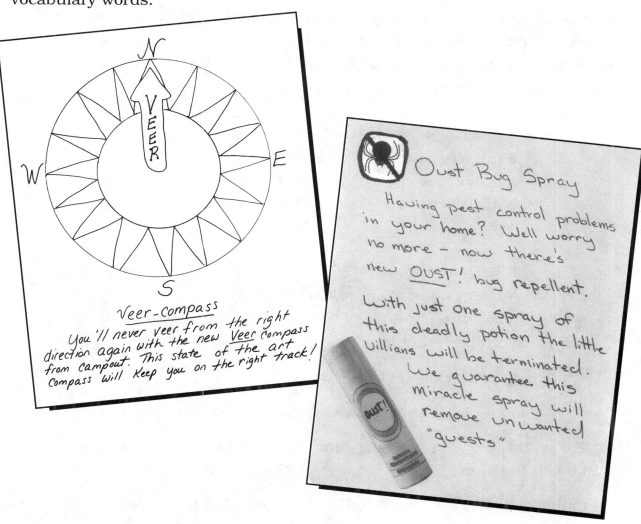

Veer-Compass
You'll never veer from the right direction again with the new Veer compass from Campout. This state of the art Compass will keep you on the right track!

Oust Bug Spray
Having pest control problems in your home? Well worry no more – now there's new OUST! bug repellent.

With just one spray of this deadly potion the little villians will be terminated. We guarantee this miracle spray will remove unwanted "guests"

Starter Sentences and Alliteration

Young writers often have trouble thinking of something to write about. As teachers, we know that a simple idea or thought can spark enough ideas to inspire a story, letter, news article, or journal entry.

Starter sentences are a great way to inspire students' writing and put vocabulary to use. I give my students a selection of starter sentences and instruct them to take one sentence and, being sure to include vocabulary words, write any one of the following:

- a monologue
- a nursery rhyme
- a poem
- a job description
- a movie review
- an obituary
- a postcard
- a TV commercial

Here are some of my starter sentences, which contain vocabulary words from our units. You may wish to construct sentences using words from your curriculum.

There is a serious **sequel** to follow.

This is about ample **apparitions** and anguished accountants.

The **gaunt,** old ghost was **haggard** from having too many horrible houses to haunt.

Jaunty jalopies carrying jaded judges stopped at **junctures.**

Parry the **premonitions** that protrude in your most **predominant** thoughts.

I like to combine this activity with a mini-lesson on alliteration. Each of the starter sentences that I give to students features alliteration, and I encourage students to experiment with the technique as they write.

Television Review

The **gaunt**, old ghost was **haggard** from having too many horrible houses to haunt. Every Monday night at 8:00 for the past seven years, Oscar, the old ghost, soared across the screens of many American TV viewers. While he provided intriguing adventures for millions of people, his stories became bland and somewhat **staid** over the years. During his first several years on the program, he portrayed a ghost who was **audacious**, **inventive**, and outlandish. Now, though, he only haunts the hallowed halls of fame where all legendary TV figures are **venerated**.

10 Syllables and Accents

Dividing words into syllables and understanding where the accent falls are very basic skills but they allow students to pronounce words correctly, understand dictionary annotations, and divide words accurately at the end of a line.

To give students practice, have them complete the reproducible on page 20 by dividing their vocabulary words into syllables and placing an accent over the syllable that is stressed. Allow students to use a dictionary if necessary.

Name ....

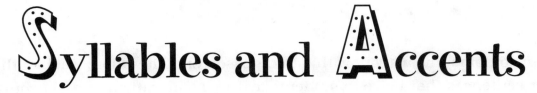 Syllables and Accents

Write your vocabulary words in the spaces below, and then divide each word into syllables. Place an accent mark over the syllable that is stressed.

Word	Syllable 1	Syllable 2	Syllable 3	Syllable 4
1.				
2.				
3.				
4.				
5.				
6.				
7.				
8.				
9.				
10.				
11.				
12.				
13.				
14.				
15.				

 Vocabulary Jeopardy

Playing Vocabulary Jeopardy is an excellent way to involve the entire class and give all your students a chance to test their knowledge, speak publicly, and compete for extra-credit points.

I use new vocabulary words to create clues for five different Vocabulary Jeopardy categories. In the "Part of Speech" category, I use the word in a sentence and students must identify whether it is a noun, verb, adjective, or adverb. In "Spelling," students must spell the word. In "Use It," they use the word in a sentence. In "Synonyms" and "Antonyms," students are given three or four clue words and must come up with the vocabulary word that is either a synonym or antonym.

To play, display the game board (page 23) with the clues (except for spelling) on the chalkboard or on an overhead projector. Students can take turns choosing and responding to the clues. You can also give each student a blank game board to fill in as you read the clues.

For all categories other then "Spelling," I allow students to refer to their vocabulary books or a dictionary.

Jeopardy is one of my students' favorites. I find that if I skip a few weeks, they'll remind me that we haven't played in a long time.

Sample Vocabulary Jeopardy

Part of Speech	Spelling	Use It	Synonyms	Antonyms
Homeless people sometimes live in <u>ramshackle</u> huts.	naive	arrogant	endless unlimited inexhaustible	meek humble unassuming modest
I have been broke for a very long time, but I won the lottery and now I am <u>solvent</u>.	epoch	naive	mild soothing dull insipid	disappoint dissatisfy frustrate
Young children find the dinosaur age a very interesting <u>epoch</u>.	niche	obliterate	nook recess	lessen diminish abbreviate
During the holidays, his <u>kindred</u> came to visit.	irascible	estrange	boring long	give a once-over restore repair

Answers:

Part of Speech	Spelling	Use It	Synonyms	Antonyms
What is an adjective?	What is naive?	Bob is very arrogant; he thinks he's smarter than the rest of the class.	What is infinite?	What is arrogant?
What is an adjective?	What is epoch?	He is so naive that he believes anything you tell him.	What is bland?	What is gratify?
What is a noun?	What is niche?	The town was obliterated by the storm.	What is niche?	What is amplify?
What is a noun?	What is irascible?	Mary and John are estranged and no longer speak to each other.	What is tedious?	What is ransack?

Vocabulary Jeopardy

In Vocabulary Jeopardy, the categories are as follows:

Part of Speech: Identify what part of speech a word is after hearing it used in a sentence.

Spelling: Spell the word correctly.

Use It: Use the word in an original sentence.

Synonyms: Name the vocabulary word after hearing synonyms for it.

Antonyms: Name the vocabulary word after hearing antonyms for it.

Part of Speech	Spelling	Use It	Synonyms	Antonyms

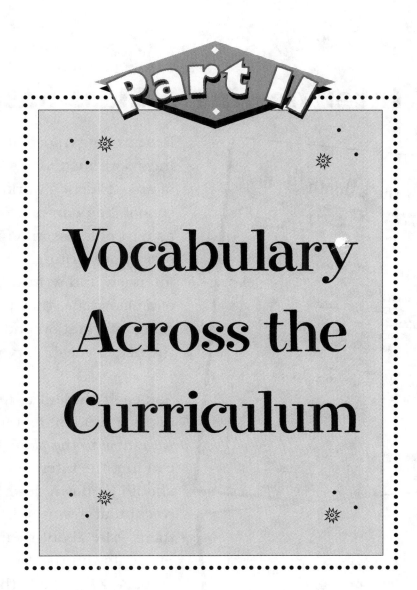

Part II

Vocabulary Across the Curriculum

plebeian · instigate · ornate · frugal · jostle · incognito · unison

12 Interviewing a Classmate

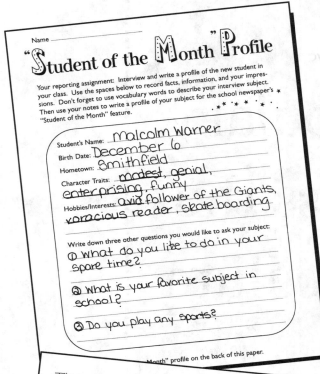

"Student of the Month" Profile

Name _____

Your reporting assignment: Interview and write a profile of the new student in your class. Use the spaces below to record facts, information, and your impressions. Don't forget to use vocabulary words to describe your interview subject. Then use your notes to write a profile of your subject for the school newspaper's "Student of the Month" feature.

Student's Name: Malcolm Warner
Birth Date: December 6
Hometown: Smithfield
Character Traits: modest, genial, enterprising, funny
Hobbies/Interests: avid follower of the Giants, voracious reader, skate boarding

Write down three other questions you would like to ask your subject:
① What do you like to do in your spare time?

② What is your favorite subject in school?

③ Do you play any sports?

Month" profile on the back of this paper.

The 2B Times
Student of the Month

Meet Malcolm Warner
Malcolm Warner moved to town last June. He is in the 7th grade and lived in Smithfield for 10 years before moving here.

Malcolm has many hobbies. He is an <u>avid</u> follower of the Giants, loves skateboarding, and is a <u>voracious</u> reader. In addition to his hobbies, Malcolm is very <u>enterprising</u>. He started a lawn mowing service, and although he is <u>modest</u> about its success, it kept him busy all summer.

Malcolm likes living here and is anxiously awaiting tryouts for the baseball team this spring.

Researching information and incorporating facts is a large part of any student's workload in school. You can use this activity as part of a lesson on research or expository writing. As students interview and write a brief profile of a classmate, they practice gathering information and reinforce the use of vocabulary words.

Ask each student to interview another student as if he or she were new to the school. As they conduct the interview, students should jot down descriptive (vocabulary) words that will help them write about their subject. Students can use the reproducible on page 27 to guide their interview. Once they have completed the interview, students can use the information to write a profile of "the new student" for the school newspaper.

An alternative to this activity is to have students create a character and then use vocabulary words to describe that character. sucess

Name ....

"Student of the Month" Profile

Your reporting assignment: Interview and write a profile of the new student in your class. Use the spaces below to record facts, information, and your impressions. Don't forget to use vocabulary words to describe your interview subject. Then use your notes to write a profile of your subject for the school newspaper's "Student of the Month" feature.

Student's Name: ....

Birth Date: ....

Hometown: ....

Character Traits: ....

....

Hobbies/Interests: ....

....

....

Write down three other questions you would like to ask your subject:

....

....

....

....

....

....

....

Write your "Student of the Month" profile on the back of this paper.

13 Horoscopes

Students are always interested in what the future may hold. Many read their horoscopes on a daily basis, looking for clues and predictions. Use their interest in astrology as the spark for a writing activity in which they become amateur astrologers. Invite them to use their vocabulary words to create a horoscope for a famous fictional, historical, or contemporary figure. If you are currently teaching interdisciplinary studies, this is an excellent way to connect language arts with social studies or science.

To get started, it's a good idea to bring in copies of the horoscope section from a newspaper or magazine so that students can read it and refer to it later. This will give students who don't read horoscopes a chance to become familiar with the section. I always point out that we read horoscopes just for fun.

In my class, I had students write horoscopes for Bert Cates, the main character in the play *Inherit the Wind.* The play is based on the trial of John Scopes, the teacher who taught evolution to his students in Tennessee where it was considered illegal. One of my students created this horoscope for him on the day before the trial.

A Horoscope for Bert Cates

Stick to your **perspective**. Be willful; anyone who will **vie** against you will fail. Avoid being **skittish**, if possible. Today is your day to be **audacious**. Keep this in mind and stay on track.

Name ....

Be an Astrologer for the Day!

Astrologers write horoscopes—forecasts of the future—based on the stars and the signs of the zodiac. Take a look at your horoscope in a newspaper or magazine. Does it give you a warning or predict that you might be successful in a new venture? Read the horoscopes for each of the zodiac signs to see how they are different and how they are the same.

Now try writing a horoscope. Choose one of the suggestions below, and write a horoscope that includes your vocabulary words. Remember to use as many vocabulary words as you can.

- Write a horoscope for a character in a book. The horoscope can warn the character about something that is going to happen later in the book or advise the character on what to do in a sticky situation.

- Write a horoscope for a famous historical figure before a major event or a prominent scientist on the verge of a discovery. For example, what might Ben Franklin's horoscope have predicted the day before he flew his kite and discovered what we now know as electricity? What might Abraham Lincoln's have said the day before he signed the Emancipation Proclamation?

A horoscope for: ....

Date written: ....

....

....

....

....

....

....

▼14▼ **Age Categories**

Sometimes how you define a word depends on who you are defining it for. Give students the example below as a reference. Then let them choose a word and define it from the point of view of a young child, a teenager, an adult, and a senior citizen. As in the examples below, students should try to use references that are appropriate for each age group. This activity encourages students to contemplate the definition of a word from many different angles.

Abashed: embarrassed or ashamed
For a child: How you felt when you were caught with your hand in the cookie jar.

For a teenager: How you felt when you realized that you left your assignment that was due today sitting at home on the kitchen counter.

For an adult: How you felt when you locked your car keys in the car.

For a senior citizen: How you felt when you forgot your doctor's appointment.

Adage: a proverb, a wise saying
For a child: Your eyes are bigger than your stomach.

For a teenager: Don't put off tomorrow what you can do today.

For an adult: Practice what you preach.

For a senior citizen: Be true to your teeth or they'll be false to you.

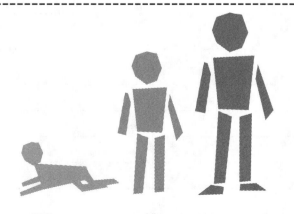

▼15 Literary Letters

Nancy Atwell, the author of *In the Middle* (Heinemann, 1987), introduced the technique of having students respond to a story or book with a letter. Letter writing is a familiar form of communication for children of all ages and therefore makes writing in the classroom more personal. It also provides an opportunity to integrate vocabulary into literature studies. The letters can be addressed to a teacher, another student, or a character in a book. Here are a few letter-writing ideas.

• Students write a letter to you. Introduce a lesson by asking students to write a letter to you that addresses an aspect of a novel or story that you'll be discussing later. For instance, you may wish to direct attention to the way the author uses dialogue to define a character. In that case, ask students to write a letter (using vocabulary words) that includes excerpts of dialogue that reveal a character's personality. Students can also use vocabulary words to describe a character or a character's actions. You can even choose vocabulary words from your list to help direct students. Letter writing is also an effective way to evaluate students' comprehension of a reading assignment. Pose a question that is related to events in the plot, and have students respond in a letter.

• Students write a letter to their writing partners about the book they are currently reading. Writing partners can respond with their own point of view.

• Students write directly to a character in a novel offering advice or comparing notes on a personal experience.

• Students write to their parents, summarizing the book they're reading and asking for feedback. Parents are usually pleased to be included in their child's learning process and sometimes write letters back to me, reminiscing about their own reading experiences, making connections to the novel we're reading in class, or just expressing delight that they are communicating with their child.

As students write their letters, they should be sure to incorporate vocabulary words into their writing.

Dear Mr. Cates,
   I am a **steadfast** believer in you innocence. I do not believe that it was wrong for you to teach us your ...ts because they weren't forced upon us. I think the law should be adapted to fit in Darwin. Thank you for not **faltering** in what you believe in.

Sincerely,
Megan

16 ▼ Vocal Vocabulary

Vocal Vocabulary is very much like show-and-tell. It allows students to *show* what they know about a word by *telling* a story to the class that illustrates the meaning of the vocabulary word. As students demonstrate their knowledge to their classmates, they also teach them the definition of the word.

For this activity, have students choose a word from the vocabulary list that is difficult for them—sometimes students need to wrestle with the toughest words before they can call them their own. Then ask them to think of a story or experience that will help to define the word. The story can be based on something they have read or a personal experience. Once students are able to connect the vocabulary word to a story, they'll be better able to understand it and to convey its meaning to others. Instruct students to use additional vocabulary words as they tell their stories.

One vocabulary word that is difficult for my students to understand and pronounce is *wanton.* Instead of placing the accent on the first syllable, my students want to pronounce the word as if it were Chinese soup. The following story, based on Edgar Allan Poe's short story "The Tell-Tale Heart," embodies the definition of *wanton.* You may wish to tell a story based on a short story you've read with your class or invent one that draws on personal experience.

Student Sample

The **wanton** behavior of the narrator in Edgar Allan Poe's short story "The Tell-Tale Heart" was frightening.

The first-person point of view in this story led the reader to believe the narrator was insane.

Here's how the story **evolved.** **Gingerly,** the narrator opened the door to the old man's room. An **oblique** slant of light shone from his lantern onto the old man's eye. He **avowed** that the eye bothered him a great deal but could not readily determine the reason.

After gazing upon the eye for several nights, the narrator decided he would not **maim** or cripple the old man, but he would kill him.

Neighbors heard odd noises from the house and called the police. The narrator confessed to the murder. His **detrimental** behavior caused the death of an innocent person.

Poe very skillfully shows how cruel and **wanton** behavior is dangerous.

Taking It Further

After students have listened to one of their classmate's Vocal Vocabulary presentation, ask them to write a sentence using the word. If the story was clear, they should be able to do this very easily.

▼ 17 Writing a Fable, Part I

Because of their simple plots and easy-to-understand messages, fables provide an ideal format for young writers to experiment with. Reacquaint your students with the genre by reading aloud some of Aesop's fables, such as "The Boy Who Cried Wolf" and "The Lion and the Mouse." After you read each story, have students identify the message or moral of the story.

Next, tell students that they're going to write a fable that illustrates a point or conveys a message and, of course, they'll need to use vocabulary words in their story.

Before students start writing, have students, as a group, brainstorm ideas for different story messages or morals. Students can outline their fables using the Write a Fable! reproducible on page 35.

Invite students to read their completed fables aloud, and ask other students in the class to state the message intended by the author. Listening to the stories will give students another opportunity to hear vocabulary words.

The Parable of the Pallid Poet
A **pallid** poet with a **pallid** pen
The **pallid** poet penned a popular poem
"Peter Piper picked a peck of pickled peppers,"
he penned
The popular poem penned by the **pallid** poet
was **plagiarized** from another **pallid** poet.
The point of the parable?
Never trust a popular **pallid** poet penning
A popular **plagiarized** poem with a popular **pallid** pen.

Name ....

Write a Fable!

When you write a fable, you'll first need to decide on the message you'd like to convey to your readers. Then invent a brief story that illustrates your point. Your story can feature human or animal characters, and you may write in prose or try a poem. Don't forget to use vocabulary words as you write.

The message of my fable:

....

....

....

....

The names of the characters in my fable:

....

....

Story summary: ....

....

....

....

....

....

....

Vocabulary words: ....

....

....

▼ 18 Writing a Fable, Part 2

Once students have completed their fables, you might challenge them to turn their tales into short stories by further developing the plot and the characters. The following story, "Unwanted Companion," was written by an eighth-grade student. The story orginated in our parable and fable writing workshop. If you've ever read Edgar Allan Poe's "William Wilson," you may recognize some similarities in plot.

UNWANTED COMPANION
by Kevin Renac

I darted to my seat as the bell rang. I noticed that there was a new kid sitting in the row next to me. He was about the same height as I am and extremely skinny. The pale kid sat at his desk, drawing in his one-subject notebook, paying no attention to the English teacher.

The extreme heat in the classroom went unnoticed by this somewhat ghostly figure, even though he was wearing jeans and a sweatshirt. I kept looking over at this kid, trying to figure out why the teacher had not introduced him to the rest of the class. Once when I was looking at him, the boy turned and grinned at me. I noticed that he was missing a tooth. The sight of his face, with that evil-looking grin, made my heart skip a beat. I knew that face from somewhere, but for some reason I could not remember where. It seemed as if my mind didn't want me to remember.

The bell rang and I almost jumped out of my seat. I had been so busy trying to figure out where I had seen the boy before that I hadn't paid any attention to the time. I quickly shoved my books in my bag and hurried to my science class.

When the bell rang, I tried to get out of the class as quickly as possible. On my way out, the kid dropped his one-subject notebook that he had been drawing in. I looked at it and saw that he had been drawing a graveyard. The tombstone in the front had an **epitaph** on it. It read:

Thomas Hubert   1979-1989

I sprinted to lunch at the sight of this name, only to find Tom waiting there for me. He followed me to all of my classes with that **cryptic** smile on his **gaunt** face.

Thomas Hubert was no longer alive. He had died in fifth grade, and it was my fault. It had been a warm, sunny day. On the way home, I thought that it would be funny to tie together the shoelaces of the skinny kid who was sitting in front of the bus. Then the bus hit a truck around the corner. The bus driver slammed on the brakes, and the bus finally came to a skidding halt. Emergency exits flew open, and kids poured from the bus. Everyone got off, except for poor Tommy Hubert, who was struggling **fruitlessly** to untie his shoelaces. Fifteen seconds after everyone else was off the bus, it exploded, and Tommy Hubert no longer had to worry about his shoelaces.

Here I am, four years later, telling my problems to a piece of paper while Tommy Hubert sits on my bed, grinning his grim smile.

19 Cloze Exercises

I find cloze exercises to be an integral part of teaching vocabulary, and I prepare one for every vocabulary unit. As in the sample on page 39, I give students a brief piece of writing in which words have been omitted. Students read the piece and fill in the missing vocabulary words. These exercises encourage students to apply critical-thinking skills as they choose words to complete the story.

You can have students practice with the sample on page 39. Allow them to use dictionaries, or provide a brief list of definitions. (See answers below.)

Once students are comfortable with the format, have them write their own cloze exercise. When they begin, I often advise my students to choose one vocabulary word and use it in a sentence. The rest of their story can grow from that sentence. Remind them to leave blank spaces for the vocabulary words.

After they've written a paragraph or two, students can exchange papers with a partner and complete the exercise written by their partner.

"Don't be stupid. Be rational, Val," Monica said.
I sighed, "Monica, you're beginning to _exasperate_ me."
"Trust me, this is the worst mistake of your life. The whole thing is going to be a complete fiasco," she warned.
"It's not like this is some _crucial_ decision that is going to affect the rest of my life," I ventured. Monica's face revealed her growing annoyance at me. I longed to fling her into an _abyss_.
"Ask him out, Val. You might be missing a great opportunity," she said.
"I don't care what I might miss. I'm not doing it."
"You're a chicken."
"And proud of it."
"Hopeless," Monica said grinning. "Completely hopeless."

Answers to cloze exercise, page 39: 1. unflagging 2. plummeted 3. attire 4. avail 5. fervently
6. proclaimed 7. stoical 8. perceptible 9. rankled 10. stint

Name ....

Fill In the Missing Word!

Fill in the blanks using the words listed below. You should be able to find clues in the text to help you identify the missing word.

attire	proclaimed	stoical	fervently	rankled
unflagging	perceptible	stint	avail	plummeted

His _____ determination to make every class with the literacy counselor
(1)
impressed everyone in class. He desperately wanted to learn to read. He was 35 years
old, and not being able to read caused him great embarrassment.

He remembered the day his spirits _____ when his young daughter, Amy,
(2)
came running to him. Dressed in her best _____ , she said, "Daddy, Daddy.
(3)
Read this. I won the writing contest at school."

He held the pages in front of his face to no _____ . He couldn't read, but he
(4)
didn't want his daughter to find out. He reacted to the composition _____, with
(5)
interest, emotion, and passion, by telling his daughter how wonderful it was.

"What did you think of the dog in the story, Daddy?"

"Oh, he was the best," her dad _____ .
(6)

"But, Daddy, he's a skinny, gaunt stray. And nobody loves him."

Her dad tried to remain _____ , but his face began to redden. It was
(7)
_____ to Amy at this point that he did not understand her writing. She
(8)
wondered if he didn't know how to read. How could that be?

Just then her brother, David, ran into the room. David was always asking his father to
sign papers. Amy watched as her father painfully formed the letters in his name.

She also read the note from David's teacher that said David was failing English. Her
father made no effort to scold David. He didn't become _____ or irritated.
(9)
That was odd.

Amy grew very sad but thought she could help. She ran to her room to get the flyer
Miss Jones handed out in school that day. A short _____ in a literacy class
(10)
would help her dad learn to read.

He said he would go and seemed relieved to know there was an answer to his problem.
Amy was relieved too.

20 ▸ Real Estate Advertising

Students can practice the art of persuasive writing by creating real estate ads for houses and apartments. You can start this activity by discussing how descriptions can impact readers. For example, ask students which sounds better: a "handyman special" or an "eyesore." The descriptions have similar meanings, but the term "handyman special" sounds much more promising than "eyesore." Read examples of real estate ads with the class, and point out the different ways houses and apartments are described.

Share the examples below with your students, and then have them use three or four vocabulary words to write a real estate advertisement for a house or apartment.

High atop a **promontory** sits this **prodigious** home. Designed with much **finesse** on the part of the architect, it will serve as a place of comfort and refuge for you and your family. It is within **proximity** of some of the finest schools, shopping, and recreation. From your **perspective** on the cliff, you will see some of the most breathtaking views of the bay in the entire state. At night, **myriad** stars make stargazing a must. If you are ready for this **milieu**, phone us at **Enterprising** Realty Company. We will be glad to take your call.

Be **audacious** and purchase this fixer-upper from **Prodigious** Realty. There are **myriad** possibilities for this house, and the price won't **incapacitate** your cash flow! In a great neighborhood with one of the **elite** school districts in the country. This one's soon to go.

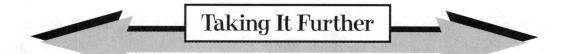

Taking It Further

When students have finished writing, post all the ads on a bulletin board. Give students an opportunity to read their classmates' ads. Then have students pick one house or apartment that they would like to live in and write a letter to a friend describing its special qualities.

Name ....

Homes for Sale

To write an effective real estate ad, you need to use words that will entice a prospective buyer. Visualize a house or apartment you would love to live in, then find vocabulary words that will help you describe it in a favorable light. Remember, your objective is to paint a picture so vivid and desirable that a person would rush to the phone to make an appointment with the realtor.

Special characteristics of the house:

....

....

....

....

Vocabulary words I can use to describe my house:

....

....

....

Advertisement:

....

....

....

....

....

....

....

Picture of the house:

▼21 Weather Reports

In an effort to help students see connections between subjects, I try to integrate our vocabulary words into the topics we're studying in social studies and geography. For example, when we were studying the Dust Bowl in social studies, I had my students imagine that they were in Oklahoma in the 1930's and then write a weather report using their vocabulary words.

There are many other times and places where weather was or is an important factor, and any of these can inspire a weather report:
- a battle (Civil War, Revolutionary War, WWI, WWII, etc.)
- a country the class is studying
- conditions encountered by explorers and early settlers
- countries struck by drought or natural disasters

Your curriculum can provide other subjects and opportunities. Touch base with the social studies teachers in your school to get a general idea of the curriculum, and then plan a lesson that integrates vocabulary and social studies.

Read the following sample to your class, and then let them try their hand at writing a weather report that pertains to a period in history.

☀ Student Sample ☀

It's **dire** weather out there today in the Oklahoma panhandle. The "blood red" dust storms are rippin' through for the 1,076 day now. These storms **defile** the natural beauty of our great state. They **chafe** the ground until only red clay and rock remain. The dust has a devil-like **mien**. We try to live like **recluses** as we fend off the dust storms, but they are **predominant** and always find a little crack in the walls to get in through. They don't give us **impunity**, even just for a minute. The storms keep pounding us to smitherines. Many people, including me, are far more than **disgruntled** about the weather. Until next time, this is Johnny Joed.

22 Literary Analysis

A friend of mine loves mystery stories. As she reads, she writes her questions and opinions of "whodunit" on self-sticking notes that she places in the book. After she has finished, she goes back to the beginning to see exactly where she began to connect the clues that were dropped by the author.

This technique is good for students to use with any kind of novel. As they read a book, students can write down any questions or comments they have about characters or plot developments, using vocabulary words to express themselves. Students can also write down any new or unfamiliar words. Later, they can share their questions with a reading partner or with the class.

A popular story in our class is *Flowers for Algernon*, which tells the story of a 34-year-old man with an IQ of 67 who is chosen as a candidate for an operation that will triple his IQ. As we read, the following questions emerged: What does IQ mean? What is a Rorschach test? Why does the author introduce the mouse named Algernon? Are there really people as smart as Charley? We stopped midway through the story and students exchanged notes with a classmate. Using the vocabulary words, they responded to one another's questions and comments.

Student Sample

Q. Why did the author introduce the mouse named Algernon?

A. I think Daniel Keyes introduced Algernon, the mouse, because he had the operation done first. The mouse was very smart and completed a maze much faster than Charley could, even though he tried very hard to **grapple** with the ins and outs of a complicated maze. It was especially funny because Algernon completed the maze in a box while Charley did it on paper. From Charley's **perspective** (67 IQ), he couldn't understand why the two mazes, with **myriad** twists and turns, were similar. In fact, when he lost the race to Algernon, he was very **perturbed**. This is the **relevance** I see right now. It may change by the end of the story.

23 Book Shorts

I created this activity after reading Maurice Sagoff's *ShrinkLits* (Workman Publishing, 1980), which I discovered one day while browsing through a bookstore. ShrinkLits are abbreviated versions of major works of literature in which the story has been condensed into a bite-size poem. I thought they were quite funny and so did my students.

Since my students enjoyed reading the short poems so much, I challenged them to write their own. We called our poems Book Shorts. As you can see from the sample below, written as a collaborative effort by two eighth graders, the students were very successful.

After you've completed a book or short story in your class, ask your students to compose Book Short poems. Students can use the reproducible on page 45 to help them include the essential points of the book. As always, ask your students to impress you by using one or two of this week's vocabulary words.

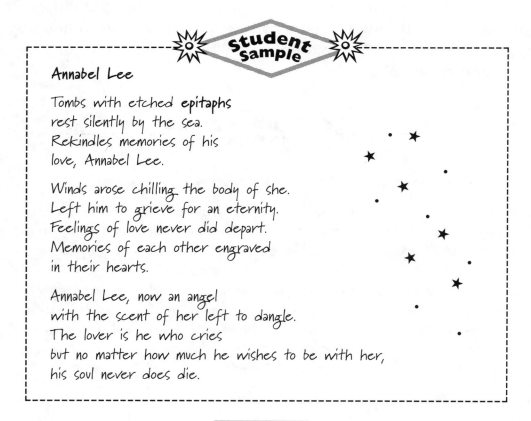

Student Sample

Annabel Lee

Tombs with etched **epitaphs**
rest silently by the sea.
Rekindles memories of his
love, Annabel Lee.

Winds arose chilling the body of she.
Left him to grieve for an eternity.
Feelings of love never did depart.
Memories of each other engraved
in their hearts.

Annabel Lee, now an angel
with the scent of her left to dangle.
The lover is he who cries
but no matter how much he wishes to be with her,
his soul never does die.

Book Shorts

Can you summarize the last book you read in a short poem? Start by thinking of the most important parts of the book. The questions below should help you remember the essential points.

Write a description of the beginning of the book.

....

....

....

Write a description of the main character.

....

....

....

Describe the conflict or problem facing the main character.

....

....

....

Describe the conclusion of the book.

....

....

....

....

Use the sentences above as basis for your Book Shorts poem. You can write on the back of this page.

24 Vocabulary Graphing

If you have students who are very visual (as I do), you'll find that having them complete a vocabulary web will help them understand and remember a word with relative ease. As they complete the web, students diagram the word by defining it, listing other forms, naming synonyms and antonyms, and using it in a sentence and an illustration.

Let students use the Vocabulary Graphing reproducible on page 47 to fully explore vocabulary words that have been giving them trouble. The opportunity to work through the word will give them a deeper understanding of its meaning. Students may find that they need to go to the dictionary to complete certain sections.

25 Vocab Diagram

Completing a Vocab Diagram (page 48) can help students brainstorm new ways to use their vocabulary. Have students select a noun—a hobby, sport, item of clothing, person, place, or animal—and place the word in a picture that illustrates it. For example, they might place the word *baseball* in a diamond or the word *dog* in an outline of a dog.

Next, have students brainstorm statements that connect vocabulary words to the noun they have chosen. In the sample here, the featured word is *baseball*, and the writer came up with "*legendary* Hall of Fame" and "*regale* with stories of famous games."

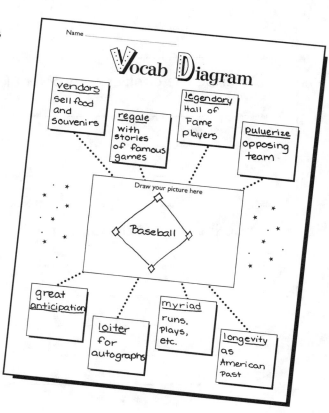

Name ....

Vocabulary Graphing

Use the vocabulary word in two original sentences.

synonyms

antonyms

_____

word

_____

part of speech

examples

other forms

Illustrate the word here.

Vocab Diagram

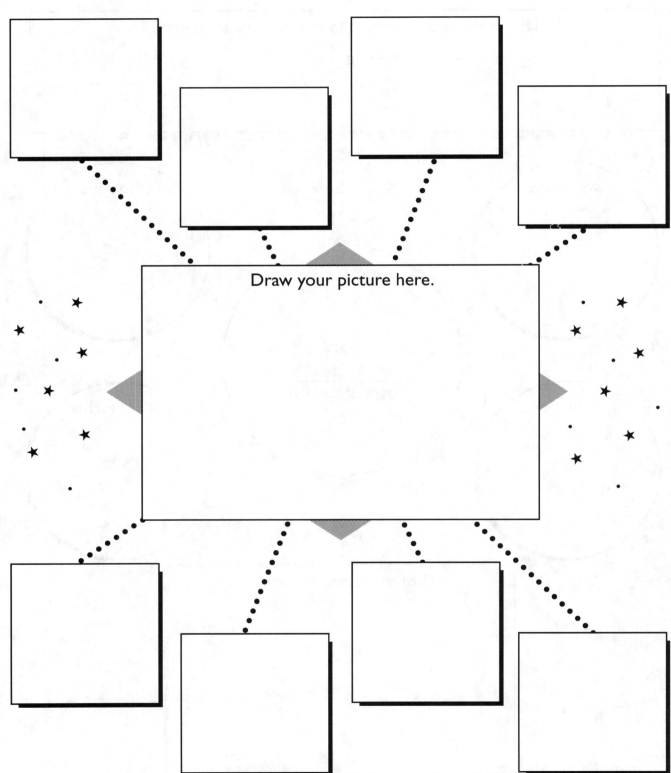

Draw your picture here.

▼ 26 Concrete Poems

Students can demonstrate their knowledge of a word by writing a concrete poem that conveys the meaning in words and pictures. In the sample below, the student has captured the meaning of *plummet* with his illustration and poem.

Have students experiment with writing a concrete poem for any word they choose. As they work on their poem, students will need to visualize how it looks and make the connection to the definition. Remind them that artwork is not a consideration—it's more important that they get the meaning of the word across to the reader, even if they use stick figures.

▼ 27 Creative Cartoons

Launch a dialogue-writing activity using comic strips. Select four or five comics from the Sunday newspaper that have dialogue and a clear storyline. After covering the text in the speech balloons, let groups of students select a comic strip to work with and create new dialogue appropriate to the action of the strip. The new dialogue should make use of vocabulary words. As students become more proficient with this activity, you might have them bring in their favorite comic strip and invite them to rewrite it.

◆28 Character Sketch

Inspire students to put descriptive words to use in a character sketch. Start by selecting either a noun or a verb and placing it in the center of the Character Sketch on page 51. Have students add adjectives or adverbs to further describe the word. When we do this activity in my class, I use the word *smile* and students add words describing the ways a person can smile.

After students have written down as many descriptive words as they can think of, they choose one word and use it in a sentence with the word *smile*. That sentence becomes the starting point for a character sketch.

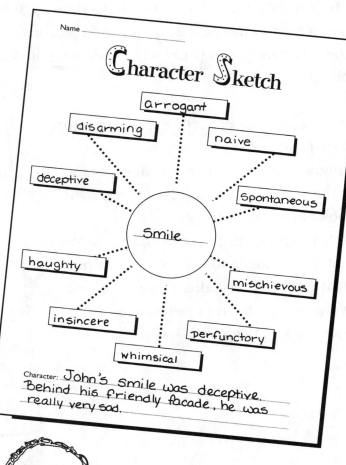

Name ....

Character Sketch

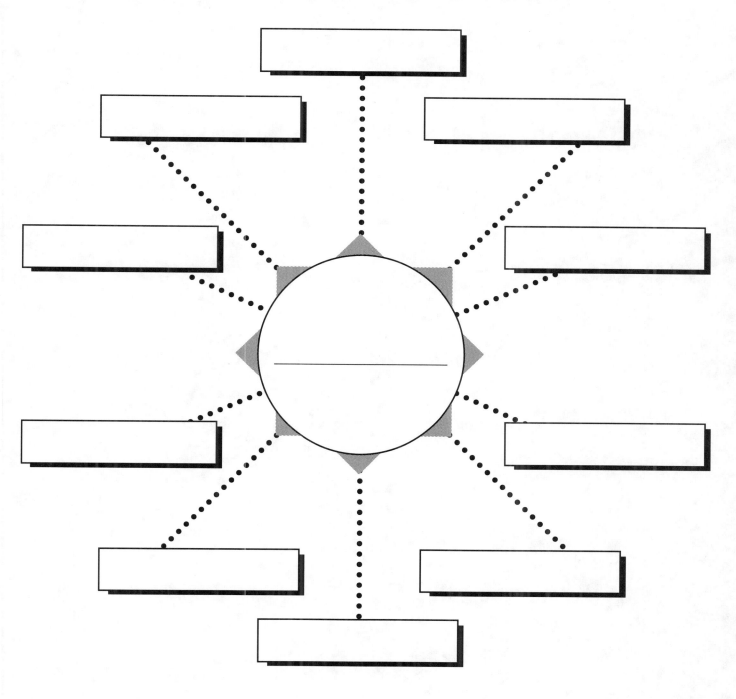

Start your character sketch here: ....

....

....

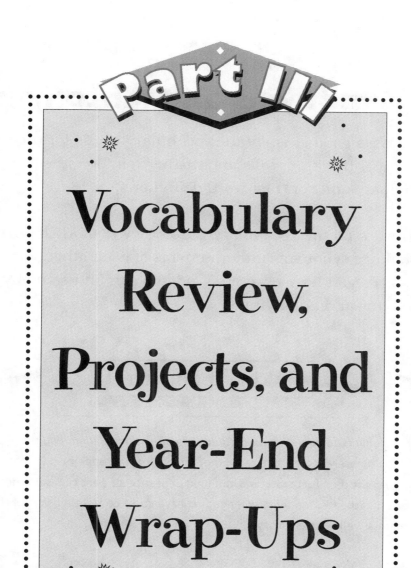

Part III

Vocabulary Review, Projects, and Year-End Wrap-Ups

plebeian • instigate • genial • premonition • adage • whimsical

 Synonyms and Antonyms

Once students have a good grasp of the vocabulary words for the year, you can sharpen their critical-thinking skills and further reinforce their knowledge by having them compare and contrast word definitions.

Have students review all the vocabulary words they've studied during the year to find words that are synonyms and antonyms of each other. Depending on the number of words you have covered, students can find as many as four to ten sets of synonyms and antonyms.

Taking It Further

After students have collected sets of synonyms and antonyms, have them use the words in a "Fortunately…Unfortunately" story. In this type of story, one sentence or part of a sentence deals with something good or fortunate and the next sentence or part of a sentence addresses something bad or unfortunate. Students will need to have good comprehension of their vocabulary words to create a well-written story.

Student Sample

Fortunately, my friend Al could be most **genial** when he wanted to be, but unfortunately, at times he made very **churlish** remarks to me. Once I asked him how a party was, and he replied, "Exactly, what do you mean by that?" Unfortunately, I **covered** at this response as I was a little **abashed** in front of our other friends. Fortunately, I did not **capitulate**, but remained **resolute** and stood my ground. Unfortunately, I knew this was a character trait he had that was extremely unpleasant. Fortunately, he apologized.

30 **What Will You Be Like in 25 Years?**

In this activity, students are encouraged to think about what they were like when they were younger, what they're like now, and what they will be like in 25 years. Using vocabulary words, students list words that describe them at each stage of life. Students can complete this activity on the student reproducible on page 56. Two or three vocabulary words in each category should be sufficient.

Once students have compiled a list of characteristics, challenge them to write a personal narrative about their life, looking back 25 years from now. Tell them that their narrative will be included in "What's Become of Your Classmates?," a book being prepared for their high school reunion. Students should use the words they have compiled in their narrative.

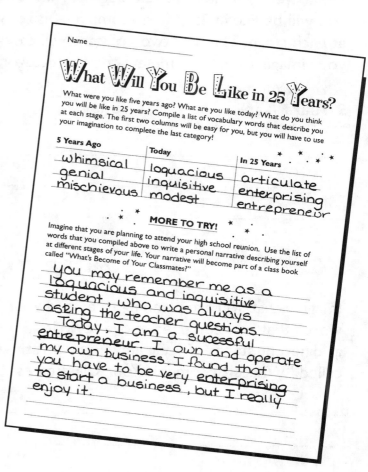

Name _____

What Will You Be Like in 25 Years?

What were you like five years ago? What are you like today? What do you think you will be like in 25 years? Compile a list of vocabulary words that describe you at each stage. The first two columns will be easy for you, but you will have to use your imagination to complete the last category!

5 Years Ago	Today	In 25 Years
whimsical	loquacious	articulate
genial	inquisitive	enterprising
mischievous	modest	entrepreneur

MORE TO TRY!

Imagine that you are planning to attend your high school reunion. Use the list of words that you compiled above to write a personal narrative describing yourself at different stages of your life. Your narrative will become part of a class book called "What's Become of Your Classmates?"

You may remember me as a loquacious and inquisitive student, who was always asking the teacher questions.
Today, I am a sucessful entrepreneur. I own and operate my own business. I found that you have to be very enterprising to start a business, but I really enjoy it.

Name ....

What Will You Be Like in 25 Years?

What were you like five years ago? What are you like today? What do you think you will be like in 25 years? Compile a list of vocabulary words that describe you at each stage. The first two columns will be easy for you, but you will have to use your imagination to complete the last category!

5 Years Ago	Today	In 25 Years

MORE TO TRY!

Imagine that you are planning to attend your high school reunion. Use the list of words that you compiled above to write a personal narrative describing yourself at different stages of your life. Your narrative will become part of a class book called "What's Become of Your Classmates?"

....

....

....

....

....

....

....

....

....

....

31 ABC Story

As you can see by many of the activities in this book, creative writing and vocabulary go hand in hand. ABC stories are a fun way for students to put their vocabulary to use while also stretching their writing skills. In an ABC story, each sentence starts with a different letter of the alphabet, beginning with the letter *A*.

I usually require students to include five to ten vocabulary words in their ABC story, so they don't have to use a vocabulary word in each sentence. I've found that it sounds forced if students try to use too many. (I also give them the option of leaving out the letters *X* and *Z*.)

As they write, remind students to incorporate the literary techniques they've learned during the year. You'll be pleasantly surprised with the quality of your students' writing. Of course, ABC stories can be developed into longer pieces of writing if time permits or if your students are interested.

Anxiously, I twisted my hands as I waited by the window.

Before I knew it, the moment I had dreaded all day had arrived.

Certainly, this wouldn't mean it was all over.

Did she really think that confronting me on my own home ground would cause me to **waver** in my decision?

 Categories

Help students recall and review all the vocabulary words you've covered during the year by using this sorting activity. Look closely at your list of vocabulary words, and think of three or four categories to group sets of words under. The words in each set should be related in some way to the category. Prepare a master list of the words that fit into your categories, and ask students to review them and then sort them into the appropriate categories.

For example, I used the categories War, Writers & Artists, and Character Traits.

War	Writers & Artists	Character Traits
scapegoat	pseudonym	disarming
turncoat	adage	captivating
rubble	sequel	frivolous
ransack	opus	articulate
impunity	metaphor	audacious
accord	denotation	pert
doctrine	edify	enterprising

For a variation, have your students come up with their own categories and find four or five words related to each one.

33 Missing Homework?

Even good students forget a homework assignment now and again. When my students don't have their homework ready for me, I give them the option of completing an alternate assignment.

Have students use three or four vocabulary words in a written exercise of any kind. They can pick the genre—journal, short story, poem, or essay. The assignment reinforces vocabulary words and the idea that homework needs to be completed on time.

34 ▼ Vocabulary Write Around

At the end of a unit, when your students are very familiar with all their vocabulary words, try this activity.

Distribute sheets of paper and instruct students to write their names at the top. Next, have students each choose a word from the vocabulary list and write a sentence using the word. Suggest that they write an intriguing sentence that someone else will be able to build on.

Have students each write their initials next to the sentence and pass the sheet of paper to the person behind them. The next writer chooses a different word from the vocabulary list and writes a sentence that builds on the first one. You can continue passing the papers around as long as time permits. At the end, return the papers to the student whose name appears at the top.

Read some of the stories aloud to showcase your students' collaborative efforts.

You can also do this exercise as a group activity. Start the story with an intriguing sentence and invite students to raise their hands to contribute to the story when they are ready.

Example:
OPENING SENTENCE: **Gingerly**, I approached the UFO.

CONTRIBUTIONS BY STUDENTS IN CLASS:

I heard the **banter** of aliens inside.

Slowly, the hatch opened, and I glimpsed a **congested** spaceship filled with control panels, flashing lights, and forms (like people) scurrying about.

Even though it sounded like a foreign language, it seemed that two of the aliens were **wrangling** about something important.

The **discordant** sounds they made warned me that something terrible might happen.

I saw a **glut** of weapons on the wall behind one of the aliens, and I became alarmed.

Soon the arguing stopped, and a panel closed over the weapons. I **groped** for the doorway and quickly exited the spacecraft.

Now, I am an **avowed** believer in UFOs.

▼35 Vocabulary Books

Your students can demonstrate their mastery of new vocabulary words by completing one of the following writing projects. Let students choose the assignment they feel most comfortable with, and give them approximately two weeks to work on it.

1. Pictionary Students select 15 vocabulary words to define in a pictionary. For each word, students write a sentence and create an illustration that depicts the word. The pictures and illustrations should demonstrate a good grasp of the word.

2. Vocabulary Advertising Brochure
Students invent 15 vocabulary-inspired products and then create product advertisements. For example, one of my students created "Bask" suntan lotion and "Minimize" diet drink. (This project is an extension of Creating a Vocab Ad on page 17).

3. Vocabulary Theme Book
Students choose a theme, such as dogs, music, or holidays, and create a book based on that theme. The book must include 15 vocabulary words, which should appear in alphabetical order. Vocabulary Theme Books are often most effective when they are written as children's books.

Assessment Rubric

Here's a sample rubric I use to evaluate vocabulary projects. I ask students to evaluate their own projects and then I evaluate them. I find that for the most part students and I will agree on the evaluation. If we disagree, it's usually the student who is tougher on his or her project.

Criteria	Points Possible	Student Evaluation	Teacher Evaluation
Use 15 words accurately in sentences.	60		
Show evidence of creativity and advanced level of sentence construction.	10		
Illustrate each sentence appropriately.	15		
Neatness. (One sentence per page; legible writing.)	10		
Cover	5		
TOTAL	100		

Seventeen Concluding Thoughts

1. Use the simpler exercises in the beginning of the book to help students think about their vocabulary words in new ways and to get them accustomed to incorporating vocabulary words in their writing.

2. Invite students to search beyond the classroom for vocabulary words. You'll find that students begin reading newspapers, magazines, and books with a new slant.

3. Model the use of new words. Use vocabulary words as you give directions in class, on handouts, and in conversations with students—every chance you get.

4. Challenge your students to use their vocabulary words in social studies, science, and even math assignments.

5. Allow time for extension activities. A brief piece of writing can be the start of an interesting, original story or composition. One of my students developed the story "Unwanted Companion" (see page 36) from a short vocabulary writing assignment.

6. Literature is a rich source of new vocabulary words. Integrate new words from books you are reading with your vocabulary units.

7. Be open to new ways of testing. Many of the writing activities in this book can serve as a vocabulary test grade.

8. Encourage students to submit their writing to magazines that publish children's writing or to enter writing contests. See resource list on page 64 for more information.

9. Ask for suggestions from your students. Often they have new and creative ideas you can use in class.

10. Don't be afraid to write with and for your students. Students like to know that even adults can learn new ways to use words and it will give your assignments more credibility.

11. Display your students' work in your classroom and keep copies of their projects and assigments to use as examples for next year's class.

12. Showcase the best of your students' work in a class anthology. This is a great project for the end of the year. Each student can select his or her favorite piece of writing to be included in the anthology.

13. Don't forget to send copies of students' work home to parents.

14. Share and exchange successful activities with your colleagues.

15. Remember—The activities in this book touch upon all of the language arts strands. Students are learning to read, write, speak, and listen.

16. Remember—Students are also using higher order thinking skills as they tackle the projects in Part II and Part III.

17. Please write to Scholastic with your comments, suggestions, and ideas.

Resources

Magazines That Publish Children's Art and Writing

Creative Kids
Prufrock Press
P.O. Box 8813
Waco, Texas 76714
Publishes poems, short stories, and mysteries written by children.

Stone Soup
Children's Art Foundation
P.O. Box 83
Santa Cruz, CA 95063
A bimonthly magazine devoted exclusively to
publishing art and writing created by kids ages 7 to 13.

Young Voices
P.O. Box 2321
Olympia, WA 98507
Bimonthly publication that welcomes fiction, essays,
and poems written by children.

Writing Contests for Kids

Children's Creative Writing Campaign
P.O. Box 999
Cooper Station
New York, NY 10276
Students 14 and under are invited to submit stories in
this annual competition.

National Written & Illustrated By . . . Awards Contest
Landmark Editions, Inc.
1402 Kansas Ave.
Kansas City, MO 64127
Annual writing contest for students ages 6–19. To receive a copy
of the contest guidelines, send a self-addressed, business-size
envelope, stamped with 64 cents to the address above.